WRN

THE WOMEN'S ROYAL
NAVAL SERVICE

Neil R. Storey

Published in Great Britain in 2017 by Bloomsbury Shire (part of Bloomsbury Publishing Plc), PO Box 883, Oxford, OX1 9PL, UK.

1385 Broadway, 5th Floor New York, NY 10018, USA.

E-mail: shireeditorial@ospreypublishing.com
www.shirebooks.co.uk

SHIRE is a trademark of Osprey Publishing, a division of Bloomsbury Publishing Plc.

A CIP catalogue record for this book is available from the British Library.

Shire Library no. 828.   ISBN-13: 978 1 78442 039 0

PDF e-book ISBN: 978 1 78442 208 0

ePub ISBN: 978 1 78442 207 3

Neil R. Storey has asserted his right under the Copyright, Designs and Patents Act, 1988, to be identified as the author of this book.

Typeset in Garamond Pro and Gill Sans.

Printed in China through World Print Ltd.

17 18 19 20 21   10 9 8 7 6 5 4 3 2 1

COVER IMAGE
Wrens fitting smoke floats to a training aircraft at a Fleet Air Arm station in 1942.

TITLE PAGE IMAGE
Wrens practising semaphore signalling at HMS *Ganges*, Suffolk 1941.

CONTENTS PAGE IMAGE
Wrens with Chief Gunnery Instructor J. Jones on the 25-yard revolver range at Rosyth in 1944. Left to right: Jose Toogood of Shanklin, Isle of Wight; Joan Collins of Manchester; Leading Wren Berthe Brokliss of London; and Marjorie Ross of Blyth, Northumberland. (IWM A 23657)

ACKNOWLEDGEMENTS
The author would like to thank the following for their kind assistance with the research and encouragement for this book:

The National Museum of the Royal Navy, Imperial War Museum, The Royal Naval Patrol Service Museum, The Royal Navy Fleet Air Arm Museum, Fiona Kay, David and Christine Parmenter, Geoff Coulton, Leo Whisstock, Campbell McCutcheon. I would like to say a big thank-you all the Wrens and their descendant families I have had the pleasure to meet over the years especially my pals – proud, former Wrens Pauline Kirkpatrick and Nia Michael.

Images are acknowledged as follows:

Getty Images, front cover and pages 53 and 54; National Portrait Gallery, page 7. Many of the images come from the Imperial War Museum and these are credited at the end of captions, identified by their 'IWM' archive numbers. All other images are the author's own.

IMPERIAL WAR MUSEUMS COLLECTIONS
Many of the photos in this book come from the huge collections of IWM (Imperial War Museums) which cover all aspects of conflict involving Britain and the Commonwealth since the start of the twentieth century. These rich resources are available online to search, browse and buy at www.iwm.org.uk/collections. In addition to Collections Online, you can visit the Visitor Rooms where you can explore over 8 million photographs, thousands of hours of moving images, the largest sound archive of its kind in the world, thousands of diaries and letters written by people in wartime, and a huge reference library. To make an appointment, call (020) 7416 5320, or e-mail mail@iwm.org.uk

Imperial War Museums www.iwm.org.uk

Shire Publications is supporting the Woodland Trust, the UK's leading woodland conservation charity, by funding the dedication of trees.

CONTENTS

PATRIOTIC SERVICE
for
BRITISH WOMEN

WOMEN WANTED URGENTLY

to enrol for the duration
of the war in the

W·A·A·C

WOMEN'S · ARMY · AUXILIARY · CORPS
and the

W·R·N·S

WOMEN'S · ROYAL · NAVAL · SERVICE

ENROL TO-DAY

Apply at the nearest EMPLOYMENT EXCHANGE for full particulars.
Ask at Post Office for the address.

INTRODUCTION: THE BEGINNING

W OMEN HAVE BEEN involved in the Royal Navy for centuries. In the seventeenth and eighteenth centuries women were employed to care for patients and work as laundresses in naval hospitals and, infamously, a number of women hid their gender to serve in the ranks aboard ships of the line. By the end of the Napoleonic Wars women had been phased out of any official employment in the Royal Navy and so the situation remained until 1854 when Mrs Eliza Mackenzie led a party of six nurses to the Navy Base Hospital at Therapia, near Constantinople during the Crimean War. But still the Royal Navy did not take women 'on board' full time until an official report in 1883 revealed the provisions for personnel ashore were sadly lacking and a certified Naval Nursing Service was established the following year with six nursing sisters being sent to Chatham and five to Plymouth. The unit did not grow greatly in size but the nurses working on hospital ships during the Anglo-Boer War (1899–1902) proved their worth yet again and in 1902 Queen Alexandra signified it was her gracious pleasure to become President of the Nursing Staff and thus the Queen Alexandra's Imperial Military Nursing Service (QAIMNS) and Queen Alexandra's Royal Naval Nursing Service (QARNNS) were created.

The Service expanded and a QARNNS Reserve of trained nurses who could be mobilised from their usual employment in civilian hospitals at short notice was established in October 1910. At the time of the outbreak of the First World War in August 1914 these were the only women serving in any branch of the Royal Navy and so it remained for the majority of the war; even in 1919 there were only eighty-one regular QARNNS nurses, assisted by just over two hundred

Opposite:
Recruitment poster for the Women's Army Auxiliary Corps and the Women's Royal Naval Service, 1918. (IWM ART PST 13195)

Dame Katharine Furse, Director of the WRNS.

Reserve nurses. During the war these nurses and those from Voluntary Aid Detachments serving under the aegis of the Admiralty Medical Department provided care at fifteen naval hospitals and aboard nine hospital ships facing the dangers of active waters all over the world. Among these was HMHS *Britannic*, sister ship of RMS *Titanic*, requisitioned as a hospital ship in 1915 and sunk by a mine in the Kea Channel off the Greek Island of Kea on 21 November 1916 with the loss of thirty lives. One of the survivors was Red Cross Stewardess Violet Jessopp, who had previously survived the sinking of RMS *Titanic* in April 1912.

Opposite:
A Nursing Sister in the Queen Alexandra's Royal Naval Nursing Service, c.1916.

Another member of the British Red Cross Society Voluntary Aid Detachment scheme was Dame Katharine Furse (1875–1972); indeed she had been involved with the scheme since 1910, formally 'joined up' in 1911 and soon became a leading light. She was a keen sportswoman, graceful, dignified, amiable, and a master administrator. She was most certainly one of those who stood out as the embodiment of the spirit of service and duty among the women of her generation. On the outbreak of war Dame Katharine was selected to lead the first VAD unit to France. Not really wanted by the military authorities, she and her team occupied a railway siding in Boulogne, where by refusing no tasks they became a laundry depot, a dispensary, and a left luggage office; they also grew flowers to make their 'rest station' attractive.

From these humble beginnings they gained a foothold that led to the VADs becoming an indispensable element in the care of the wounded in active service theatres during the First World War. The prominent surgeon Sir Frederick Treves was to comment when inspecting them, '30,000 ministered to in five weeks … a fine piece of Red Cross work.' On her return to London in 1915 Furse was promoted to Commandant in Chief of Voluntary Aid Detachments but she was constantly frustrated by the lack of power she had as she tried to introduce reforms in administration and living conditions for VADs attached to temporary military hospitals.

The War Office had not been keen to involve women beyond qualified nurses in any of the services. Only after years of pressure and the demonstrably good practice and valuable services rendered by independently raised women's uniformed organisations before and during the conflict did the War Office begin to consider women joining them; and it was only after such losses had been sustained by the men fighting at the front that they gave any serious consideration to the number of valuable men who were currently deployed on home or non-active service. Once this realisation dawned, Whitehall sanctioned the creation of the Women's Army Auxiliary Corps, which was raised under the ethos and banner of 'Free a Man for the Front!' This first official British army corps for women to serve both at home and abroad in support of the fighting forces was established in

1917 and the first WAACs proceeded to France within a couple of months of its inception.

Dame Katharine had taken an active interest in the new women's branch of the army and had wanted to get involved. Offering help to Neville Chamberlain, who was the Director of National Service at the time of the formation of the WAACs, she had been ignored and not being able to find out exactly what was going on she wrote directly to Sir Reginald Brade, the Permanent Under-Secretary of State for War, pointing out her desire to learn more about the scheme and expressing her concerns that the creation of the WAAC had been done without consultation with the experienced leaders of extant women's branches and organisations.

Meanwhile, the Admiralty, who were already employing women who lived locally at its naval establishments in

WRNS Director Dame Katharine Furse addressing officers and ratings of the WRNS who had passed through their preliminary training at Crystal Palace and were shortly to be drafted to various stations, 1918. (IWM Q 18716)

non-uniformed clerical work, had been perturbed by the wider debate driven by the Ministry of National Service, who were suggesting there should be a single organisation for women to serve in all government departments – both civil and military. Envisaging the difficulties that could arise if it had to compete with other government departments that were also increasing the numbers of women employed by them, the Admiralty set about establishing its own women's corps along the model of the WAAC.

Dame Katharine was already disenchanted and had resigned from the British Red Cross Society, with a number of her senior staff colleagues, in November 1917. Soon afterwards she was offered the post of Director of a new naval organisation that that was to be raised from scratch and she took many of her old 'tried and tested' team from the Red Cross with her.

The challenge of setting up a brand new unit *her way* was right up the street of Furse. Among her stalwart staff colleagues who joined her to help establish and lead this new venture were Mrs Winifred Daykins and Miss Mary Cane, who became Assistant Directors, and Miss Edith Crowdy, who was appointed Deputy Director. Edith was joined by her sister Isobel a short time later. Rachel Crowdy, the third sister, with whom Furse had joined the VADs back in 1911, was the only one to remain with the BRCS. Dame Katharine, Miss Edith Crowdy and Mrs Tilla Wallace set about drafting regulations, but it was Crowdy who became deeply involved in the implementation of the new regulations for the Wrens. Dame Katharine would write of her: 'she instilled confidence in everyone by her bold but calm behaviour.' It was this whole team of driven and efficient women of action that gave the Wrens such firm foundations when it began.

The first decision to be made was what to call the new unit. Practical and sensible names had to be ruled out when they considered the resulting acronyms; suggestions like Women's Auxiliary Naval Corps or Women's Auxiliary Naval Service would have led to countless problems and provoked ribald humour. The Women's Royal Naval Service (WRNS or Wrens) was the only one that really worked. Although it has to be said the Admiralty were not keen to allow the 'Royal', they did reluctantly agree to it.

Opposite:
Recruiting
poster for the
Women's Royal
Naval Service by
Joyce Dennys,
1918. (IWM ART
PST 2766)

WOMEN'S ROYAL NAVAL SERVICE
APPLY TO THE NEAREST EMPLOYMENT EXCHANGE

ANCHORS AWEIGH!

THE WOMEN'S ROYAL Naval Service was 'born', officially, on 23 November 1917 when Dame Katharine Furse was formally appointed Director, a rank equivalent to Rear Admiral, under the superintendence of the Second Sea Lord, Vice-Admiral Sir Herbert Heath. Miss Edith Crowdy was appointed Deputy Director on the same date. The First Sea Lord then formally wrote to HM King George V for Royal Assent on 26 November 1917:

> Sir Eric Geddes, with his humble duty, begs to inform Your Majesty that the Board of the Admiralty have under consideration the possibility of substituting women for men on certain work on shore directly connected with the Royal Navy, and as a result of full enquiry, it is recommended that a separate Women's Service should be instituted for the purpose.
>
> It is submitted for Your Majesty's approval that the Service should be called THE WOMEN'S ROYAL NAVAL SERVICE, and that the members of the Service should wear a distinctive uniform, details of which will be submitted to Your Majesty for approval in due course.
>
> The Service would be confined to women employed on definite duties connected with the Royal Navy and would not include those serving in the Admiralty Departments or the Royal Dockyards or other civil establishments under the Admiralty.

The King was pleased to signify his approval and the Wrens were rubber stamped on 28 November 1917.

From the moment Dame Katharine received her appointment she was off out of the starting blocks. On

Opposite:
A WRNS motor driver, 1918.
(IWM Q 19656)

Newly joined
Women's Royal
Naval Service
recruits report for
training at Crystal
Palace, London.
(IWM Q 18708)

the same day that Sir Eric Geddes sought Royal Assent, a temporary Headquarters Office was opened at Central Buildings, Westminster, and the Assistant Directors were soon appointed to take charge of the five departments of Administration (Winifred Daykins), Personnel (Mary Cane), Inspection and Training (Isobel Crowdy), Recruiting (Muriel Currie) and Medical (Dr Annie Forster). Preparations were made, uniforms designed, rules and regulations set in place. The rapid development of the Wrens necessitated the transfer of their headquarters to 15 Great Stanhope Street on 7 January 1918 and recruiting began in earnest with a call for 10,000 women to join. Those with qualifications to become officers were told to apply to the Professional Women's Register, Queen Anne's Chambers, The Broadway, Westminster; those who wished to join the ranks were urged to apply through employment exchanges or women's recruiting huts.

It was pointed out in the literature and reportage that all officers in the Wrens would be 'mobile' and as such must be prepared to serve anywhere they were sent; the ratings, however, would be both 'mobile' and 'immobile' (those based in their home and who would be working at a nearby base). The vexed question of accommodation having caused much delay in recruiting, a special appeal was made to women living in their own homes at the great naval bases of Britain to come forward and join.

The remit of the Wrens had become a wide one and was working towards the substitution of naval ranks and ratings in branches including all the Royal Navy, Royal Marines, Royal Naval Reserve, Royal Naval Volunteer Reserve, and Royal Naval Division in the United Kingdom, and the Royal Naval Air Service – in fact almost any sphere of naval work normally done by men, save manning a warship.

The uniform for all ranks in the WRNS was described, when it was announced in the press, as 'an attractive kit' but it was admitted that it was still not quite ready and subject to some modifications due to difficulties obtaining certain materials. Truth was the Treasury balked at the WRNS officers wearing gold lace 'because of the wasting of gold', which the WRNS were willing to accept as this was 'the prerogative of the men'. Thus, officers would be dressed in a navy blue coat and long skirt, with gilt Royal Navy buttons and ranks worn upon the cuffs in rings of Patrick's blue; a black tricorn hat with the Royal Navy officer's cap badge except with the laurels in Patrick's blue, a white blouse and collar and black tie, which would be purchased out of grants made to officers.

The ranks corresponding to Petty Officers wore a pilot jacket with black Royal Navy buttons and a skirt cut in neat, straight lines. They were also planned to wear a navy blouse. Rank and file would be issued a blue serge frock coat of good

Members of the WRNS parading before Mrs Vera Laughton Mathews (later appointed Director of the WRNS for the Second World War) outside Crystal Palace, 1918. (IWM Q 18907)

Women's Royal Naval Service (WRNS) ratings undertake rifle practice at Crystal Palace, London, 1918. (IWM Q 18705)

navy serge, a blue linen sailor collar and a navy overcoat. Strong boots and stockings would also be supplied. It had originally been planned for the Wrens to wear round sailor's caps with cap tally bearing the initials 'WRNS' in gold but this was changed to a stitched cap with a brim made in navy cloth with the tally worn on that instead. Following the form of the Royal Navy dress regulations a white cap cover was also introduced, to be worn during the summer months.

On 26 January 1918 the first training course for officers in the WRNS was opened. These were held in London with the assistance of Queen Mary's Army Auxiliary Corps lecturers, until the WRNS College was set up at Ashurst, near Crystal Palace. A new entry establishment for ratings was also set up, along with a WRNS unit with stores ratings, writers, despatch riders and drivers under Miss Vera Laughton at Crystal Palace itself in February 1918.

The appointment of senior officers to naval bases and stations had begun on 18 January 1918 and by mid-March 1918

A member of the WRNS practising flag signalling at Crystal Palace, 1918. (IWM Q 18900)

there were just over a thousand ratings on duty or reporting for service. The general organisation of the WRNS was on a territorial basis of areas, termed divisions, each one of them administered by Divisional Directors or Deputy Divisional Directors. Coinciding, to some extent, with the principal naval bases, the seven major divisions, under Divisional Directors, were Portsmouth, Chatham, Devonport, London, Scotland, Ireland and even the Mediterranean. In fact, the first WRNS unit to serve abroad was despatched to Gibraltar; there was soon another in Genoa. Headquarters of the Mediterranean Division were established in Malta and a small party of officers had set out shortly before the end of the war to investigate possible bases in Egypt where sub-divisions had been planned for Ismalia, Alexandria and Port Said. Another group had also departed ready to start a base at Bizerta on the African Coast but the end of the war in November 1918 saw them recalled while still on their way out from England.

Lesser divisions under Deputy Divisional Directors were those of Cardiff, Harwich and the Humber, while independent officers bearing the rank of Principal were put in charge of the companies in the Liverpool and Tynemouth districts and of the groups of air stations (formerly naval) on the East Coast.

WRNS officers at Portland, 1918.

The naval stations or companies included in the above numbered some two hundred, while about thirty air stations (formerly RNAS) were staffed with ranks and ratings WRNS. After the creation of the Royal Air Force in 1918, Wrens posted to air stations formerly naval were transferred in due course to the Women's Royal Air Force, while those wishing to remain in the WRNS were moved to a naval establishment at the earliest opportunity.

The personnel of the WRNS consisted of Officers, Subordinate Officers and Women. WRNS Women could be promoted to the rating of Leader, Section Leader and Chief Section Leader, equivalent for purposes of discipline to the naval ratings of Leading Seaman, Petty Officer and Chief Petty Officer.

There were two branches of officers in the Service: administrative and non-administrative. The badges for their respective ranks were the same, but non-administrative officers were not given a rank higher than that of Deputy Principal. By the end of 1918 there were 123 administrative officers and 163 non-administrative officers. Many of the non-administrative officers replaced male naval officers working on decoding while others were charged with secretarial and certain technical duties. The total number of 'ratings' at work was close on 5,000, divided into eight categories of employment.

The period of enrolment for WRNS was for twelve months or 'for the duration' of the war, and was similar to that of the WAAC and WRAF. The training course for administrative

Despatch carriers of the WRNS delivering messages to a drifter, 1918. (IWM Q 19661)

officers covered a period of four weeks, some thirty to fifty being entered in each session at the WRNS College. Training included physical drill, lectures and naval tradition, structure etiquette and the organisation of the WRNS, with practical work on the paper side of the latter. An examination was set but the final result of training depended more on character and general fitness than on any paper test. Non-administrative officers were trained in decoding and deciphering at the Signal School, Portsmouth, while other technical training of a confidential nature was given to those required to replace naval officers in special posts.

Wrens working as ship's clerks on board HMS *Essex*, Devonport, 1918. (IWM Q 19762)

Chief Section Leaders and Section Leaders were initially trained by Forewomen of the WAAC until suitable WRNS trainers were appointed. They learned the theory of the category of their work, management of women, the use of forms, hygiene, drill, discipline, games, and were 'imbued with the necessity for tact and courtesy when dealing with the women working under them, as well as with the men with whom they would be working.'

With regard to training for ratings, decoding clerks were trained over a three-week course at the Signal School, Devonport. Prospective senior writers would go to Crystal Palace for a four-week course, to improve their shorthand and typing, while typists received a six-week course at the depot hostel.

In the domestic category, four-week training courses for cooks were held at Portsmouth, Devonport, Chatham and London. Motor drivers, who had already trained before enrolment, had two weeks of special coaching in London at the WRNS Motor School. Telephonists received three weeks of training; wireless telegraphists were given a three-and-a-half-month course; and there were other technical trainings of a confidential nature.

Once qualified, Wren ratings would be given a trade category denoted by blue non-substantive trade badges worn

Opposite: Storewomen of the WRNS sorting ships' lamps, Lowestoft, 1918. (IWM Q 19733)

on the right arm, mid-way between shoulder and elbow; in the case of section leaders and senior section leaders, these badges were worn on the upper lapel of each collar.

WRNS BADGES

Crossed quill pens – Clerical and Accountant Branch
Scallop shell – Household Branch
Three-spoked wheel – Motor Drivers and Garage Workers
Arrow crossed by a lightning flash – Signal Branch
Crossed keys – Storekeepers, Porters and Messengers
Envelope – Postwomen, Telegraphists and Postal Workers
Star – Miscellaneous
Crossed hammers – Technical Workers

The accommodation for members of the expanding service saw the establishment over fifty hostels, run with WRNS officers in charge. Domestic quarters exclusively for Wrens were also allotted, or hutments erected at extant naval establishments. Where a hostel was not available, 'approved lodgings' recommended by the Ministry of Labour would be used. In some ports entire hotels became Wren

WRNS ratings sail-making on board HMS *Essex* at Devonport, by Stanhope Forbes, 1918. (IWM ART 2621)

accommodation, such as in Portsmouth where both the Lion and Miller's Hotels were taken over. All members of the WRNS so accommodated would have a fixed rate of 15s 6d for officers and 14s for ratings deducted from their wages every week if their conditions of service did not include free board, lodging and washing. Dame Katharine, who had campaigned for better conditions for VADs, took pains to ensure Wrens' accommodation was regularly visited and reported upon by officers from the WRNS Department of Inspection.

WRNS ratings gather in their recreation room at Miller's Hotel in Portsmouth, 1918. (IWM Q 19712)

The central drafting hostel was set up in five houses on Courtfield Road, South Kensington. Wrens would be accommodated there while awaiting their draft and transfer from one division or station to another. Women attending courses in London would also be accommodated there; indeed the hostel itself also became a training centre for some courses. The Women's Active Service Club, opened in September 1918 at 48 and 49 Eaton Square, was also a popular place for WRNS officers and ratings if they were passing through London.

The overall well-being of the women of the WRNS was the responsibility of the Medical Assistant Director, working under the Admiralty Medical Department, but while serving at naval establishments or stations the health of the women would be supervised by the Naval or RAF Medical Officer in charge. Voluntary Aid Detachment Nursing Members were also attached to sick bays in the larger hostels and at the dressing stations provided at centres where work might cause exceptional fatigue or risk of injury. A convalescent home for officers was also provided at Checkendon Court, a Tudor mansion in the South Oxfordshire Chilterns.

Their work was cut out for them in a totally unexpected way after the outbreak of Spanish 'flu in January 1918, a deadly pandemic that would more kill more people worldwide than died as casualties of the First World War. Working in harbour areas, the Wrens were directly exposed to the virus as it entered the country at various ports and a number were stricken by the illness and died as a result. However, influenza did not claim the life of the first Wren to die in service: Section Leader Cook Mrs Alice Mary Flannery (aged 39) died two days after having an exploratory operation for cervical cancer at the Women's Hospital, Castle Gate, Nottingham on 9 August 1918.

It was to be the sinking of the Holyhead-bound mail steamer RMS *Leinster*, torpedoed by the German submarine *UB-123* just outside Dublin Bay on 10 October 1918 that resulted in the first Wren to lose her life at sea while on active service. The ship sank in just eight minutes and over 500 lost their lives in the sinking – indeed, it proved to be the greatest ever loss of life in the Irish Sea. Three Wrens were on board: two were rescued, but tragically Wren Clerk (Shorthand Typist) Josephine Carr of Blackrock, Cork, Ireland, went down with the ship, and her body was never recovered. She was just nineteen years old. Her name is recorded on Plaque 31 of the Plymouth Naval Memorial.

During the First World War the number of Wrens reached a peak of 438 officers and 5,054 ratings. They could be found working in a host of jobs, from sailmakers, painters, cleaners, wood turners, fitters, cooks and bakers to drivers of both motor vehicles and motorcycles, porters for light and heavy victuals, garage workers, telephonists and clerks. At Immingham they worked adjusting naval gyroscopes; in draft offices they mapped sections for use abroad and for flying schools in the UK; and

A group of bakers of the WRNS at Royal Naval Barracks, Chatham, 1918. (IWM Q 19784)

notably in Battersea Experimental Workshops they also drew, traced and helped prepare designs for all kinds of new military machines and guns. Wrens drove staff cars and lorries, cleaned out the boilers of trawlers, maintained and repaired ships' lamps, searchlights, hydrophones and gas masks, and oiled and cleaned torpedoes on the Humber, constructed wire nets for use against enemy submarines and even cleaned the floats and mines that were to be attached to them. Some even undertook the priming of depth charges. They took over wireless work at listening stations and worked as coders and decoders, where they kept the same watches as the men and took their turn on all night work. At the RNAS Anti-Aircraft Corps the telephonists continued throughout the numerous raids by both Zeppelins and Gotha bombers, passing through the orders for gun-fire and barrage to the gun stations. In fact it was the three officers serving at Granton Naval Base, Edinburgh, who decoded the signals telling of the surrender of the German Fleet in November 1918. The end of the war, however, heralded the beginning of the end of the WRNS, at least for the time being.

In May 1919 the WRNS Honours List, the only one for them during the war, was published. It included forty-nine officers and twenty-two ratings, all of whom had been awarded an array of medals from the CBE and MBE to the BEM. At the Great Peace Day Parade in London on 19 July 1919 the WRNS detachment had their place and proudly marched

through the streets of the capital to cheering crowds. It was during this parade that they marched past King George V as he stood upon a dais in front of Queen Victoria's monument outside Buckingham Palace. Shortly after passing His Majesty they passed the contingent of some of the Royal Navy's most senior officers who, to a man, spontaneously applauded them. The Wrens on parade that day never forget that moment. Despite many tributes and plaudits recorded at the time, many of them considered it was the greatest thanks they received for what they did in the First World War.

Dame Katharine fought for the preservation of the Navy's women's branch but the scheme was dropped by order of the Board of Trade and her suggestion of an unpaid WRNS volunteer reserve, run along the lines of the Girl Guides, was also declined by the Admiralty. The Admiralty Fleet Order announcing the gradual demobilisation of the WRNS was sent out on 19 February 1919, final demobilisation papers were dated September 30 and the WRNS ceased to exist on 1 October 1919.

Dame Katharine was not to be beaten: she wanted to maintain links between her girls and give them support if

they needed it in those post-war years in very much the same way that men set up their Regimental Associations or ex-servicemen's charity organisations such as The Comrades of the Great War or the British Legion. On 20 January 1920 she called a meeting at her home, 112 Beaufort Street, Chelsea, to discuss representation and on 21 February 1920 a meeting was held at Portsmouth Blue Triangle Club and the WRNS Friendly Association was founded and by March they had adopted its popular name – The Society of Wrens, finally adopting the collective noun for the bird associated with their Branch of the Senior Service. The inaugural dinner saw 190 ex-Wrens gather at Miss Ethel Martha Royden's Club on 19 November 1920, a General Meeting to officially set up the AOW was held the following day and the first Association of Wrens committee met on 16 December 1920. Local branches were encouraged to form in the old divisions and even a magazine, *The Wren*, was started with Vera Laughton as editor. The purpose of the magazine was to keep all the members in touch and foster the continuation of the comradeship they had shared during the war.

One last picture 'for the record' of the officers and ratings of the WRNS at Portland, 1919.

WOMEN'S · ROYAL · NAVAL · SERVICE

H.M.S.

join the
Wrens

AND · FREE · A · MAN · FOR · THE · FLEET

THE SECOND WORLD WAR

WHEN THE WINDS of war began to blow again in the mid-1930s an initial attempt to create a Women's Royal Naval Reserve, after due consideration by the Special Sub-Committee of Imperial Defence, was high-handedly rebuffed as 'deemed not desirable'. In September 1937 Dame Katharine Furse, the Director of the WRNS in the First World War, wrote to the Admiralty Board to offer the services of the Association of Wrens in the event of war emergency. The need for the Wrens again became increasingly pressing and in July 1938 the Admiralty minuted that there was indeed a need to form a Women's Royal Naval Service and the first public announcements for initial recruitment appeared in November 1938. Out of all three women's services raised during the First World War the WRNS was the only one of the units raised again in the 1930s to retain its original name.

Mrs Vera Laughton Mathews was appointed Director of the WRNS in April 1939. Born in Hammersmith in 1888, Elvira Sybil Marie 'Vera' Laughton had served in the WRNS during the First World War; indeed she had enlisted the day the first announcement was made and had been chosen from the first Officer's Training Course to form the first WRNS unit. Always a keen and able leader, she had kept her links as one of the leading lights of the Association of Wrens and was prominent as Commissioner of Girl Guides and Skipper of the Sea Ranger branch of the Girl Guides during the inter-war years.

The adverts recruiting for the WRNS in 1939 were outlined in the HMSO publication *National Service: A Guide to the Ways in which the People of This Country May Give Service*, in which it stated the WRNS were

Opposite:
Recruiting poster
for the WRNS,
c.1942. (IWM ART
PST 8286)

initially looking for about 1,500 women aged between 18 and 50,

> … to take the place of Naval and Marine ranks and ratings in Naval establishments upon secretarial, clerical, accounting, shorthand and typewriting duties; and domestic duties as cooks, stewardesses, waitresses and messengers… anyone who is interested in this service should send her name and address to the Secretary of the Admiralty (C.E. Branch), Whitehall London S.W.

In the first instance the revived WRNS would only be raised in large naval ports on the 'immobile' basis, in that officers and ratings would only be accepted who could undertake to serve from their own homes in the Portsmouth, Plymouth, Chatham and Rosyth areas.

The steep learning curve for those who established the WRNS so well back in the First World War provided a legacy of both firm foundations and seamarks for those reviving the WRNS in 1939 and they really did hit the ground

New recruits for the revived WRNS learning to give the Royal Naval salute at a training base 'somewhere in Southern England' in July 1939.

WRNS Director
Mrs Vera Laughton
Mathews
inspecting
a parade of
Wrens at RNAS
Hatston (HMS
Sparrowhawk),
Orkney, Scotland,
26 May 1942.
(IWM A 9109)

running. The WRNS was organised into two categories: one was 'specialised branch', which would cover office duties, motor transport and cooks; the other was 'general duties branch', for stewards, storekeepers and messengers. All ranks would be uniformed.

WRNS RANKS AND ROYAL NAVY EQUIVALENTS, 1939–1945	
Ordinary Wren	Ordinary Seaman
Wren	Able Seaman
Leading Wren	Leading Seaman
Petty Officer Wren	Petty Officer
Chief Wren	Chief Petty Officer
Third Officer	Sub Lieutenant
Second Officer	Lieutenant
First Officer	Lieutenant Commander
Chief Officer	Commander
Superintendent	Captain
Commandant	Commodore
Chief Commandant	Rear Admiral

WOMEN'S
ROYAL
NAVAL
SERVICE

Join the

WRENS

and free a man

for the

FLEET

A WRNS recruiting leaflet from the Second World War.

Initially, the WRNS volunteers were to be given training and after serving a probationary qualifying period would be enrolled for four years. Wrens would be required to attend at least forty-eight drills of 1 hour each year at the naval or marine depot where they enrolled. Drills were to consist of twenty-four 2-hour instruction periods in the evening or an intensive training period of one week. There was no pay for Wrens in peacetime but each member completing the forty-eight drills would receive 10 shillings annually towards expenses.

Thousands of women answered the appeal for volunteers; many of them were those who had served in the first incarnation of the WRNS and now wished to join again, bringing their daughters with them, but in those early months of 1939 there was no general mobilisation. Great consideration was given to the skills the women already had acquired from civvy street and recruits were selected and were destined to be placed or entered into specialist training where they were thought to fit best. Thus the foundations of the new WRNS were laid well and were ready to welcome the mass of volunteers in 1939 and 1940, as well as those brought in by the conscription of women in 1941.

Volunteer recruits accepted for the WRNS would have been sent for a preliminary medical examination and would then go home to await their call-up papers. The length of time a volunteer would have to wait would depend on the number of vacancies in the area she was to work in. When the papers eventually arrived a travel warrant would be included to take her to a preliminary training depot, often on a Wednesday because old Navy tradition was that incoming and outgoing drafts were on that day.

Upon arrival a further medical examination would be carried out and a few preliminary tests would be conducted to ensure the recruit was placed in the right division for her experience and aptitude. At the Central Training and Drafting Depot in London there were six main divisions named after six famous seamen, namely: Nelson, Effingham, Drake, Howe, Beatty and Collingwood. In addition there were two Raleigh divisions for the training of cooks and stewards.

The recruit would also learn a little about routine and discipline over the ensuing two days. For fourteen days she would be a probationer, wearing navy-blue overalls with coloured tabs to denote her division and would be able to leave if she wished or could be released from the WRNS if found unsuitable.

At this first depot the recruit was taught the basics of service life and discipline. Even her language and terminology would change, for she was now part of the Royal Navy: her room became her 'cabin', the dining room was 'the mess' and the floor the 'deck'. Her work would be divided into 'watches' with 'divisions' held in the Assembly Hall and Holy Communion in a small chapel every day. Lectures would be given on naval procedure, ranks and

Sleeve badge of a Petty Officer Wren.

A working party of Wrens scrubbing out a boat at Plymouth, 1942. (IWM A 7032)

A Wren collects her towels, shoes, shoe brushes and a tie from the Supply Ship at HMS *Eaglet*, 1942. (IWM D 7305)

badges along with passive defence and a variety of skills pertinent to service life. Physical fitness and drill were also key aspects of training – by the time the trainee departed she must have proved herself fit and capable of marching and be able to give the correct naval salute. Team games were particularly encouraged.

In addition to their practice training cooks worked in three watches of twenty trainees under a Chief Petty Officer (who would hold a domestic science degree) to learn how to cook for large and small numbers on gas, steam and electric appliances.

During her first week the prospective Wren would only be allowed three hours' 'shore leave' during the first week, but this was extended each week she stayed the course; there was also a weekly film show and dance. The trainees were also allowed to smoke and 'generally amuse themselves' in their fo'c'sle.

After fourteen days' probation, if found satisfactory, candidates would then be enrolled into the WRNS and would be issued with their top kit, with 45s for the purchase of personal kit such as pyjamas or nightdresses, brassieres or bodices, hairbrush, sewing kit, boot brushes and polish, handkerchiefs, spare laces and navy or black knickers 'closed at the knee' – all of which could be purchased from Navy stores. A kit upkeep allowance of 2s 8d was paid to ratings to keep their kit in good order and buy their own replacements if necessary from this sum.

STANDARD UNIFORM KIT ISSUED TO WRNS RATINGS

1 overcoat – navy blue, double breasted, six buttons, two side
    pockets without flaps
1 raincoat – navy-blue waterproof twill, single breasted with
    belt, vertical side pockets, raglan sleeves
2 jackets – serge double breasted, six black anchor buttons
2 skirts – navy serge, six-gore
4 shirts – white poplin
9 collars – white
1 tie – black
2 pairs shoes – black leather, no toe cap
3 pairs stockings – black lisle
1 hat tricorn – CPOs and POs only
1 cap – blue cloth – ratings below PO only
1 cap ribbon – naval uniform pattern, ratings below PO only
Or
1 Royal Marines cap badge and red flash – for ratings in
    RM establishments
1 pair gloves – navy woollen
1 bag – utility
1 toothbrush
Badges as appropriate

At the end of three weeks the trainee would leave for her first placement at a naval base or establishment or would proceed to a specialised training school for her category.

The variety of WRNS categories soon on offer to recruits was truly remarkable. To give an idea of the diversity the list includes the following (the length of the specialist training course is shown after the job title): AA Target Operator (3 weeks); Air Mechanic Electrician (24 weeks) – during the whole of this course there were tests and examinations of the student's comprehension and practical work culminating in a 30-hour inspection; AM Transcriber (3 months), Coder (4 weeks), Torpedo WRNS (10 weeks). Good skills in mathematics were a requirement for entry to this category but with that, deft skills with their

Wireless
telegraphist
Wrens in training
at HMS *Unicorn
III*, Crescent
House, Dundee,
January 1942.
(IWM A 7024)

finger was just as important. In peacetime the training of
the torpedoman was spread over years, not weeks. Wrens
would spend their first four weeks of specialist training in
this area mastering the theory of electricity, learning about
the tools for the job and receiving instruction on how to fit
and pack deck tubes. Next she was taught about the care
and maintenance of underwater weapons and would attend
lectures on torpedo firing circuits, buzzers, lighting systems
and electrics. Finally the Wren learnt how to assemble,
service and disassemble the torpedo itself and mastered the
mechanism of the depth charge.

The list goes on: Radio Mechanic (36 weeks); Photographic
Assistant (11 weeks); Meteorological (6 weeks at a naval air
station – here the Wren is trained by the Meteorological
Office and learns to make routine weather observations,
judge height, types of cloud, record temperatures and estimate
visibility); Parachute packer (5–12 weeks – working with the
Fleet Air Arm and requiring 'strong wrists, great accuracy

and patience' the Wren would not only work on packing, maintenance and repair of parachutes but also worked on the emergency rubber dinghies); and Boat Driver (3 weeks).

In 1941 WRNS officer training took three weeks; intakes of cadets varied between twenty and thirty every week. In that same year Special Duties Linguist training began at Wimbledon; the first WRNS personnel arrived at Station 'X' Bletchley Park in February 1941.

The WRNS despatch riders provided a valuable service and acquired a formidable reputation for their endurance and tenacity in overcoming any difficulty of hazard they met in the course of their duties. Devotion to duty became synonymous not just among the DRs but was also extended to the Wren plotters during operations such as the evacuation from Dunkirk and the Dieppe Raid and across the WRNS branch of the Royal Navy during the war.

A fine portrait study of a newly passed out Wren ready to set out on her service life.

The first Wrens to serve overseas were sent to Singapore early in 1941 under the charge of Second Officer Betty Archdale; every one of her thirty Wrens was a Chief Wren Specialist Wireless Telegraphist Operator. They were safely withdrawn before the fall of Singapore and completed their overseas service in Africa. During the course of the war Wrens served in many commands over most of the world, including South Africa, India, Ceylon (Sri Lanka), Egypt, France and Belgium.

Wrens played many roles during Operation *Overlord* in 1944. During the build-up they were involved in Operation

The cadre of Wrens under the command of Second Officer H.E. Archdale shortly before they left for Singapore, 1941. (IWM A 3257)

Fortitude, to deceive the Germans into thinking the landings would be made elsewhere. Their work listening to, decoding and recording intercepted messages in the 'Y' Stations across Britain and at Station 'X' helped build a massive intelligence of the enemy's actions. WRNS and WAAFs worked together on the D-Day plot in Portsmouth Combined Headquarters. Wrens acted as confidential book and chart correctors, working night and day to update maps, for example, to show channels cleared by minesweepers. They also worked as despatch riders, drivers, stores and office staff. Indeed, between 25 May and 5 June 1944 WRNS officers acting as censors in ports dealt with some 400,000 letters.

And let us not forget the cooks that kept so many fed. In the Portsmouth Combined Headquarters, for example, there were three wardroom messes, each of which served 800 meals in every 24-hour period. In the WRNS mess alone there were 1,200 meals a day and a two-course supper provided in five shifts for between 2,030 and 2,300 personnel.

After the successful D-Day landings on 6 June 1944 the work of the Wrens did not end there; their support continued at the headquarters and bases. The hundreds of Wren ship mechanics, working with Royal Navy ship mechanics in the ports along the South Coast, were on duty night and day to repair damaged craft when they made their way back from the

Normandy beaches. As the British and Allied forces pushed into France the WRNS followed too; the first landed on 15 August 1944 to work at Courseulles-sur-Mer and more followed, often making the journey from Portsmouth to Arromanches seated on the floors of large trucks with only their kit bags to offer some comfort. None of them would forget the sights they witnessed as their transport rumbled through the war-shattered towns and villages of Normandy.

September 1944 saw the WRNS at its apogee, with 74,635 officers and ratings in 90 categories and 50 branches. As the

A Wren Visual Signaller uses a flash lamp to receive and send messages to ships at this Fleet Air Arm station, somewhere in Scotland, 1943. (IWM D 13389)

Wrens sampling the Christmas pudding at Greenock, Scotland, 19 December 1942. (IWM A 13392)

course of the war changed in favour of the Allies the WRNS began to be wound down again. Categories of their work were reduced and the main release scheme for wartime Wrens began in May 1945. Each Wren was allotted a release number and informed when to expect her demob. For her release from service she was given a clothing grant, coupons, a gratuity based on her length of service, a civilian identity card and ration book. She would also be given a discharge certificate, which could be used as a reference for civilian employment, and two months' paid leave between leaving her unit and finally leaving the WRNS. Unlike at the end of the First World War, though, in 1945 there were no plans to disband the WRNS.

It should not be forgotten, however, that the war took its toll too. At sea, the sinking of SS *Aguila*, one of twenty three merchant ships that formed Convoy OG71, resulted in the loss of twelve Cypher Officers, ten Chief Wren Specialist W/T Operators, and a Naval Nursing Sister en route to Gibraltar when they were torpedoed by a U boat in the early hours of 19 August 1941. Another tragic loss at sea occurred on 12 February 1944 when nineteen Wrens went down with the SS *Khedive Ismail* when she was torpedoed en route from Mombasa to Colombo.

Left: WRNS craftswomen painting a motor-launch (ML 195) at HMS *Tormentor*, Southampton, c.1944. (IWM A 19496)

Below: Commonwealth War Graves headstone marking the grave of Second Officer Anne Jago-Brown WRNS serving at HMS *Midge*, Great Yarmouth, Norfolk. She was killed during an air raid upon the town on 18 March 1943 and lies buried in nearby Caister Cemetery. She was thirty-three years old.

The WRNS suffered further losses during air raids and as a result of accidents in the United Kingdom. Among the major incidents were the deaths of ten Wrens serving with HMS *Daedalus*, RNAS Station, Lee-on-Solent, when their hotel received a direct hit during an air raid on 14 September 1940. In a similar incident five Wrens serving with HMS *Midge* were killed and thirteen rescued after their quarters at Great Yarmouth received a direct hit on 18 March 1943. On 31 May 1943 a party of WRNS ratings were returning from a dance to HMS *Blackcap*, RNAS Stretton in Cheshire, when the driver of the 3-ton truck they were travelling in lost control, crashed into a field and overturned in a ditch killing eight WRNS in the accident. During the Second World War a total of 102 Wrens died and 22 were wounded serving their country.

Overleaf: Demob paperwork, Employment Certificate and coupons for Leading Wren Betty Bray, who served between April 1942 and February 1947.

S. 458. (Established—December, 1944.)

W.R.N.S. EMPLOYMENT CERTIFICATE

Name (in full) _Betty Gwendoline BRAY_

Rating on discharge (in full) _Leading Wren._

This rating has been employed in the W.R.N.S. from

17th April, 1942 to _5th February 1947_

on _Messenger duties from 17.4.42 until 18.11.42_
Writer (General) duties from 19.11.42 until Released

Character during service † _Very Good_

General efficiency during service † _Average_

Efficiency on discharge † _Average_

SPECIAL REMARKS.—Power of command, intelligence, initiative, energy and any
other qualification not otherwise recorded ‡ :—

A reliable and hard working
Leading Wren who has had a good
Service record. Capable of good
work without supervision.

R Shepshanks.
FIRST OFFICER, WRNS FOR COMMODORE. ~~Captain.~~

† To be recorded as for men—see Art. 610, K.R. and A.I., clauses 3 to 7.

‡ To be completed in the establishment from which discharged to shore, or to Depot as a
preliminary to discharge to shore.

N. 13338/44

(18/12/44) (501) Wt. 18556/D7851 50m 7/45 S.E.R. Ltd. Op. 671.

THIS CARD IS NOT TRANSFERABLE. IT MAY BE
USED ONLY ON BEHALF OF THE PERSON
NAMED ON THE COVER.

NATIONAL RATIONING
LEAVE OR DUTY RATION CARD R.B. 8A.
(72 Hours)

How to use this card

1. In order to buy any food that is rationed you must produce
this card, and the person serving you will detach the appropriate coupons. You must not detach coupons yourself ; if you
do they will be useless.

2. This card is intended to cover a period of 72 hours and for
the rationed foods there are three coupons for meat, one for
bacon and ham, one for butter and margarine, one for cooking
fats (including lard and dripping) and one for sugar. If the
period of leave or duty does not exceed 48 hours, one meat
coupon will be detached by the Issuing Officer.

3. Half a meat or bacon coupon may be used to buy a cooked
meal of rationed meat or bacon in an hotel, restaurant, café,
teashop, etc. The half coupon must be detached from your
ration card by the person serving the meal.

4. If whilst on leave or duty you are supplied with any of
the above rationed foods in kind from your unit or ship, the
Officer issuing your ration card will detach the appropriate
coupons and you will be unable to purchase such food from
civilian sources.

5. You must spread your coupons over the full period of your
leave and of your journey out and back. No fresh card will be
issued to you. The card ceases to be valid at the expiration of
your leave or duty as indicated by the date entered opposite 3 on
the front cover of this card.

6. If your leave or duty is extended you must take this card
with the document authorising the extension of leave or duty to
the local Food Officer, who will issue an Emergency Card to
cover the remainder of your leave or duty.

S. 1586 (W). (Established—January, 1945)

ORDER

(W.R.N.S., Retired and Reserve ...

To _B. G. Bray_

Leading Wren .... (Rank or R...

Official Number. _35153_

*Insert:—
"Class A" or
"Class B" or
"Compassionate"

1. You are being discharged from Service ...

2. The date of your discharge will be ...

*Delete as
necessary.

3. You have been granted leave as follows
   *...........days' foreign service leave expir...
   *_50_ days' resettlement leave
   *...........days' transfer leave } expiri...

4. You are free to take up civil employment ...
   you are being released in Class B, is the ...
   (See Note 3.)

Delete para. 5 if
a "Class A" or
"Compassionate"
Release.

†Insert Exchange
nearest to
permanent
address.

5. If you are a Class B release you will b...
   as a ....(Ins...
   tion No...............) and you are to r...
   †..................within 7 days of ...
   to take up your reconstruction employm...
   if you wish at any time after the date ...

6. You may wear civilian clothing at any ...
   wear uniform after the date of your di...

7. Your home address is noted in official ...
   German
   _R. A..._

8. Your Service Certificate if you are a ra...

9. You should carry this Order with you ...
   .... when required.

DISCHARGE OFFICE
W.R.N.S.
5 FEB 1947
R.N. BARRACKS
DEVONPORT

Note 2—Class A consists of married women ...
   length of war service under the Pla...
   between the defeat of Germany and ...
   Class B consists of individuals speci...
   reconstruction work.

Note 3.—Information regarding the reinstate...
   in leaflet R.E.L.5.

Note 4.—While you are on leave you should ...
   Office from which you were paid.

(72283) Wt. P.309/2680 10m pads 11/45 Lev. Gp. ... 41-2558

Form S. 1599

DUPLICATE—To be sent to Officer or Rating.

P.O.S.B. ACCOUNT PARTICULARS	
H.M.S. _Drake II_	
No.	_341 £3_

WAR GRATUITY & POST WAR CREDIT OF WAGES
to be deposited in the POST OFFICE SAVINGS BANK

SURNAME (in block letters)	BRAY, Betty Gwendoline,
Full Christian Names	Leading Wren 35153
Rank or Rating and Official No. ...	H.M. Coastguard Store,
Permanent address (give full postal address) ...	Gerran Haven, St. Austell, Cornwall.
Date when amount is due to be deposited in the Savings Bank	31st October, 1946

	Service From	To	Unpaid Time Days	Net reckonable Service Months	Reckonable Rank or Rating	Rate per month	Amount Payable £ s. d.
War Gratuity	17. 4. 42	15. 8. 46		52	Leading Wren	8/-	20 - 16 - =
Post War Credit of Wages in respect of Service as a Rating after 31-12-41.	17. 4. 42	30. 6. 46	1586 (Days)	—	per day 4d.	25 - 12 - =
				Total amount of War Gratuity and Post War Credit £			46 8 =
				Less deduction in respect of outstanding charges on pay account, etc. £			
				Amount for deposit ... ... £			46 - 8 - =

Date of dispersal to leave ...
Date of termination of Foreign Service leave (if any) ...
Date of release ...

A.S.... for Captain(S),
Signature and rank of Certifying Officer

Date _13th January, 1947._

S. 1596.   (Established April, 1945).

RELEASE DOCUMENTS.

Name ...*BRAY*......*Betty Gwendoline*...

Rank or Rating *Ldg Wren*........ O.N. *35153*......

Address ...*Farar House   St Austell*......
(To be completed by Holder).   *Cornwall*   *5/2/47*

The following documents have been supplied to you for your release or discharge, and are enclosed in this envelope :—

Order for Release ;

Railway Warrant ;

Ration Card for 14 days ;

Application for National Registration, Clothing Coupons and Ration Book ;

Application form for Medical Treatment
(not to uninsured officers);

Health Insurance Contribution Card
(not to uninsured officers);

Label for return of uniform
(not to officers or W.R.N.S.) ;

S. 450.   Officer's Certificate
(not to W.R.N.S. Officers);

Civilian Clothing Warrant
(not to W.R.N.S) ;

S. 1006.   Income Tax Form ;

S. 1595.   Officer's Claim for War Gratuity
(if not already completed).

NOT TO CLASS B.

Form for claiming Disability Pension ;

Pamphlet "For Your Guidance" ;

Application for Reinstatement in Civil Employment (R.E. 1) ;

Leaflet with regard to Reinstatement Rights (R.E.L. 2).

CLASS B ONLY.

Leaflet with regard to Reinstatement Rights (R.E.L. 5).

In addition, you should have your History Sheet and Trade Certificate, if you are not an officer or in the W.R.N.S. If you have been dispersed from a R.N. Barracks or the P.S.C.D., Lowestoft, you should have an Unemployment Book. If you have not been dispersed from a Barracks or the P.S.C.D., Lowestoft, an Unemployment Book will be sent to you.

NELSON WOULD HAVE BEEN PROUD

ENTWINED IN THE history of the WRNS in the Second World War are some remarkable achievements and acts of gallantry performed by members of the service – too many to mention in this volume. It is worthwhile, however, to pause and reflect on just some of the stories, of which anyone, including the greatest of those who served in the Senior Service, would be justly proud.

The first Wrens to distinguish themselves in the Second World War were those who served on the roads of the land rather than the sea – the despatch riders. The first four Wren despatch riders entered the Admiralty in 1939 and were attached to the Intelligence Department. Led by Wren Petty Officer Whitney they carried messages through the bitter winter of 1939–40 and soon established a reputation for getting through, no matter what. They earned their spurs all right and other naval establishments such as Portsmouth and Liverpool soon acquired their own Wren despatch riders. During significant operations such as Dunkirk or Dieppe the WRNS despatch riders would work in eight-hour watches day and night and a 'stand-off' period would not be known.

One of the despatch rider Wrens was Third Officer Pamela George, who was carrying urgent messages to the Commander-in-Chief's office during a heavy air raid on Plymouth when a bomb exploded nearby and completely wrecked her motorcycle. Unperturbed she ran half a mile to carry a message to Admiralty House while high explosive and incendiary bombs fell all around her. On her arrival, having delivered her message, she immediately volunteered to go out again. She was awarded the British Empire Medal for her gallantry on that day.

Opposite: Recruiting poster for the Women's Royal Naval Service, 1944. (IWM ART PST 8453)

Wren despatch riders photographed in 1941. Among them were a number of well-known pre-war competition riders. (IWM A 2828)

In a special order of the day of 22 August 1942 issued in Portsmouth, Admiral W.M. James wished to praise the ten WRNS despatch riders serving there who had, over the previous fortnight, covered 10,000 miles and delivered numerous immediate and important despatches. He singled out some for specific praise; two of these were Tustin and Harris:

Leading Wren Tustin led convoys in thick mist and over strange roads to their destination and PO Wren Harris did valuable service in carrying a staff officer over dark and difficult routes. Both these Wrens were 21 hours on duty without a pause. PO Wren Harris had previously covered 250 miles in seven and a half hours' running time, 100 miles being in the dark and apart from two hours' sleep was on that occasion on duty for 26 hours. During the week before the D-Day landings there were unprecedented demands on the Wren despatch riders who were riding from 5.00pm to 3.00am, having a couple of hours' sleep, would ride all the next day until 8 or

9.00pm then were called out again after supper to ride until two in the morning, sometimes covering 200 miles in a single watch.

Although it is true to say that WRNS did not serve in action aboard battleships they did actually serve at sea in dangerous wartime waters across the Atlantic and all over the world, carrying out communications work, cyphering and coding aboard troop ships such as the famous *Queen Mary* and the *Queen Elizabeth*. In a letter of praise to WRNS headquarters, which sums up so much about how WRNS were trained and how they conducted themselves, the US Army Port Commander at the Hampton Roads Port of Embarkation in Virginia USA wrote:

This port has shipped nearly 2,000 women passengers on the *Empress of Scotland* during the past three months. These WAC Army Nurse Corps and American Red Cross women have had an excellent example of the highest type of 'women in war' given by the WRNS detachment on this vessel. The neat, fresh appearance, alert, earnest manner and quiet, unobtrusive efficiency shown by these five WRNS must have made a material impression upon the women passengers just starting out on their

Boom Barrage Wrens anti-aircraft gun crew being inspected in their gunpit by the Royal Navy Commander in charge of the gun sites at Felixstowe, September 1942. (IWM A 21881)

A Wren radio mechanic prepares for a flight to test newly fitted equipment at Royal Naval Air Station Hatston, 1942. (IWM A 9115)

war venture. This detachment offers an exemplification of the adaptability of women to perform wartime duties that require attention to duty, strict discipline, in confining and often dangerous surroundings in a calm, unassuming manner.

A number of WRNS drafts suffered their vessels being torpedoed while proceeding overseas or while in transfer from station to station; only one serious loss occurred when

British Naval Officers and Wrens at work in the plotting room at Chatham. (IWM A 28255)

a draft were lost going from Kilindini in Kenya to Ceylon. That said, there were numerous gruelling experiences for Wrens stuck in lifeboats in foreign waters, unsure when or if rescue would come.

Back in the UK, a little-known unit of the Wrens were the Operational Boom Defence Wrens. In her book *Blue Tapestry* Vera Laughton Mathews, the Director of WRNS from 1939 to 1946, recalled the Wrens on these duties at Felixstowe in Suffolk:

> That is what they were called, but it was really secret operational work which had little to do with boom defence. It was outdoor work of a heavy manual nature and apart from the senior officers in charge was entirely carried out by Wrens. Big strong girls were chosen and when I saw them in the field in bell bottoms and navy blue jerseys they looked like Amazons.

Their secret work entailed the inflation of large latex balloons with hydrogen gas which would carry a bottle of liquid nitrogen; this would be released over the sea to drift towards enemy shipping, aircraft or territory and on impact with the ground, deck or overhead cables would burst into flames.

Wrens at a naval exchange dealing with the immense network of naval private lines at the Royal Navy signal station known as 'Signal City' at Greenock, Scotland, October 1942. (IWM A 13717)

It was dangerous work and a number of the girls suffered burns when the balloons caught fire before they left the ground. The thing that was particularly unique about these Wrens was, however, that they were trained and authorised to operate and fire the guns for the defence of the station because otherwise it would have meant bringing in men for that purpose alone. This they did until the employment of servicewomen in the firing of lethal weapons was discussed inter-departmentally and prohibited.

It is not widely known that Wrens also worked with the Fleet Air Arm (FAA). The roles within the Arm were varied from the regular support categories of secretarial, supply and cooks as well as trade categories that included the exacting jobs of parachute packing and meteorology. In fact there were soon so many WRNS ratings engaged in various duties with the FAA in November 1942 that it was decided to form the Maintenance (Air) Branch, which encompassed work from aircraft washers, battery chargers, and plug cleaners to electrical and air frame ratings. At its height in 1944 there were 1,581 Wren air mechanics. Trained WRNS even flew on missions with the Fleet Air Arm working on radios and on aerial reconnaissance; the first of the flying Wrens to do so 'as part of her regular duties' was Leading Wren Pat Lees (aged twenty-one), a radio mechanic who was flying in 755 Squadron Lysanders during September 1942. By the end of 1945 there were also thirty-nine trained WRNS air radio officers responsible for the technical aspects of all radio equipment in aircraft and on the ground.

The Wrens working in signals and plotting rooms are also too often forgotten. They worked for Naval commands and Royal Naval Patrol Service depots all around Britain but the hub of it all was the plot in Portsmouth Combined Headquarters where the Wrens and the WAAFs worked as a perfect team to update the large-scale map of the English and French coasts that lay out before them. In this room came all the unfiltered information from both sides of the Channel as well as from ships and many other authorities. The map was criss-crossed with coloured lines indicating convoy routes, with coloured cardboard squares and code

Three WRNS
River Pilots at
Plymouth Naval
Base studying
charts before
sailing, 1944.
Left to right:
Pat McGinnis,
Pat Turner and
Patricia Downing.
(IWM A 24948)

names and numbers showing the positions of landing craft and their escorts. Numerous engagements and battles were directed from this plot, the signals also being coded and transmitted by WRNS signal officers and wireless/telephone operators. Over 450 Wrens were on duty night and day in the Signals Office; indeed, the communications at Portsmouth Combined Headquarters were staffed by Wrens. They saw the whole of D-Day unfurl and many of them worked voluntarily for fourteen-hour stretches. More than 5,000 signals were sent out from there on 6 June 1944. In both the plotting room and signals room, accuracy and speed were absolutely critical, the work could never stop and frequently the strain was acute.

Wrens trained as home harbour boat crews taking over boat as all WRNS crews in all roles be they coxswain, stoker or deck hands, day and night, winter and summer, foul weather and fair. Theirs were the boats that patrolled the harbours and ran supplies, mail, senior officers' launches and liberty boats to shore from ship and back again. A letter written by a seventeen-year-old Plymouth Wren revealed some of the experiences of Wrens crewing liberty boats:

The dramatic cover artwork for the popular *Women of Glory* story book 'for young adults' that recounted some of heroic acts of Wrens during the Second World War.

> I am pretty sleepy at the moment as I was on duty last night and we didn't get to bed until 2.00am, and our first trip was 6.30am this morning.
>
> We were doing liberty trips all night out to the destroyers in the Sound. The last trip at midnight was the worst. It was blowing pretty hard and we had to take eighty men out and many of them were not sober.

Leading Wren Nina Williams (née Marsh) and Ambulance Driver Joan Westerly of Coventry after their investitures with British Empire Medals for bravery and devotion to duty, at Buckingham Palace, 13 March 1941.

Before we even had started four of them went over the side. Luckily it was moonlight so we had no difficulty in fishing for them with a boathook. I just saved a fifth from going over by catching him by his gas mask, just as he was disappearing.

Third Officer Audrey Coningham was one three Wrens among 1,135 passengers aboard the submarine depot ship *Medway* when it was torpedoed while it was sailing from Alexandra to Haifa on 30 June 1942. Hundreds were suddenly in the water and having found the scramble nets full on the nearest rescue vessel she swam towards another. After she had been swimming for around 15–30 minutes she saw two men clinging to just one life belt. One of them was trying to help the other, Leading Seaman Leslie Crossman, who had injured legs and his head kept disappearing beneath the water. Third Officer Coningham had learned life saving at her convent school so she confidently took off her own life belt and put it on the drowning man saying 'Lie still. You'll be alright. Trust me.'

Her selfless act enabled Crossman to stay afloat until he was rescued and he eventually made a good recovery, returned to service and went on to earn a DSM for a later

BEM heroine
Wren Elizabeth
Booth, 1944.

act of bravery. Third Officer Coningham was recommended for an Albert Medal but she was denied the award because she was judged a strong swimmer, she had not put her life at risk and a witness to her bravery had helped in the rescue so the award she received was a Mention in Despatches but she wore it with great pride. It is believed she was the only women to be decorated for bravery at sea during the Second World War.

During air raids and seaborne attacks WRNS boat crews were also exposed to many dangers and would be called to help bring in wounded sailors if convoys in roads and channels near to them were attacked. In one instance on 18 September 1940, six Focke-Wulfs raided Dartmouth and sank a collier, the SS *Fernwood*. Leading Wren Chadwick and Wren Kneebone were crewing a naval launch nearby and immediately went to assist; they helped the crew to safety, administered first aid to the injured and were praised for their 'courage and efficiency' throughout. This incident was not unique and other boats crews did similar work during the course of the war.

Some of the most significant acts of bravery by Wrens occurred during air raids on Great Britain. Among them was Leading Wren Nina Marsh, despite being wounded in the back and elbow during an air attack on Royal Naval Air Station, Ford, on 29 August 1940. The oil refinery had been hit; petrol tanks and a storage hangar were set on fire and the sick bay was badly damaged. Leading Wren Marsh made light of her injuries and gave invaluable assistance in dealing with the wounded in the sick bay shelter trench under the most trying circumstances. She refused to give in until all casualties had been dealt with and evacuated, then she was herself sent to hospital.

Wrens from HMS *Vectis* at work on the dock at Cowes on the Isle of Wight, 1945.

Then there was 24-year-old Wren Elizabeth Glen Booth of Leeds: when a Swordfish aircraft crashed at the Crossaig Bombing range near her remote Scottish airbase of Machrihanish on 18 November 1943, she drove an officer to the spot and even though the explosions inside the aircraft were scattering burning debris and petrol around she saw the Fleet Air Arm aircraft's observer had been thrown onto the ground, so with complete disregard for her safety she ran to him, dragged him clear of the main wreckage and beat out the flames on his burning uniform with her bare hands then tore the smouldering clothing from him. She then drove him the 9 miles along a tortuous route to the doctor.

Both Wrens were awarded the British Empire Medal for their gallant conduct.

Serve with the Royal Navy in the **WRNS**

THE POST-WAR YEARS

O N 8 MAY 1945 the Board of Admiralty sent a message of thanks to the WRNS to all stations at home and abroad, which concluded:

> The loyalty, zeal and efficiency with which the officers and ratings of the Women's Royal Naval Service have shared the burdens and upheld the traditions of the Naval Service through more than five and a half years of war have earned the gratitude of the Royal Navy.

It was recognition that was well deserved and meant so much to the Wrens that had served. The WRNS was still going to exist in peacetime but because the war emergency had passed it would only be required in a far reduced size of some 3,000 for mainly admin and support roles at Royal Navy establishments and RNAS stations at home and abroad. Many Wrens were happy to take their demob and return to civvy street but many of them kept in touch with their fellow Wrens and carried on that special bond they had known while 'in the service' and the Association of Wrens flourished.

Her duty done, Dame Vera Laughton Mathews retired and she was succeeded as Director by Dame Jocelyn Woollcombe in November 1946. Wollcombe would see one of the most important developments for the WRNS since its inception, as on 1 February 1949 the WRNS became a permanent part of the Royal Navy. In peacetime there were twenty-four categories that were open to WRNS ratings that ranged from clerical, household and medical to radar plotters, air mechanics and radio maintenance. It was stressed that ratings in all categories shared equal opportunities for promotion to Officer, and that

Opposite:
A 1960s recruiting brochure to the WRNS.

HMS *Dauntless*, Theseus Division, Burghfield near Reading, 1946.

all Officers, except a few with specialist qualifications, were to be selected from serving ratings.

After a successful nucleus unit was established in London in 1951, the Women's Royal Naval Volunteer Reserve was established in 1952 and attached to RNVR Divisions in London, Severn, Tay, Forth, Clyde, Sussex, Humber, Mersey, Tyne, Solent and Ulster. On the Reserve's twenty-fifth anniversary it was recorded that there were 900 officers and ratings in the WRNR.

Throughout the post-war years the question of why Wrens could not have full equality was regularly asked at senior military and political levels, particularly because if Wrens were supposedly considered capable of holding any post why shouldn't they fight in battle? A Ministry of Defence Study Group was set up in January 1974 to 'identify and redefine the role of the WRNS for the next ten years and beyond.' The findings of the group suggested integration was the key to the future of the WRNS and made suggestions such as changing the training and structure of the WRNS to enable them to do more demanding jobs. The final passing-out parade of the WRNS Officers Training Course at Greenwich was held on 19 March 1976 before moving to train with the RN at

BRNC Dartmouth where the first joint course was begun in September 1976.

In 1981 the New Entry Training Establishment, HMS *Dauntless*, Burghfield closed after thirty-five years and having trained some 30,000 Wrens. Initial training of Wrens transferred to HMS *Raleigh*, Torpoint, where, with supervision from WRNS officers, the Wrens would train alongside new entrant Royal Navy ratings. It was the beginning of the end of the WRNS as a separate arm of the Royal Navy.

Defence cuts saw the need to maximise the effective use of all naval personnel on shore to support the Fleet and drove on the integration process as both male and female ratings received identical training. This was proved to be effective during the Falklands crisis in 1982 when WRNS personnel were moved at short notice to take over operations at home naval bases to release men for duties at sea. It would be almost ten years later, in 1990, when falling recruitment for the Royal Navy raised the need for Wrens to go to sea and as a result the first cadre of twenty volunteer Wren officers and ratings joined the crew of HMS *Brilliant*. It was to be the beginning of the end of the WRNS as an arm of the Royal Navy. In 1993 the WRNS was disbanded and 4,535 women were fully integrated into the Royal Navy, able to serve on Her Majesty's Ships at sea at all ranks and rates.

In the twenty-first century, women serving in the Royal Navy face the same dangers as their male comrades, are on active service, and are being decorated for their gallantry. In 2009, Medical Assistant Class 1 Kate Nesbitt was decorated with the Military Cross at Buckingham Palace for her gallantry in Helmand, Afghanistan. She is the first woman serving in the Royal Navy to receive it and only the second woman ever to receive the award. Her citation states: 'Under fire and under pressure her commitment and courage were inspirational and made the difference between life and death.' The legacies of fortitude and spirit of the WRNS are alive and well in every woman who serves in the Royal Navy and long may it remain so. Rule Britannia!

A post-war example of an arm badge for a Leading Wren.

FURTHER READING

Anon. *The Wrens: Being the story of their beginnings and doings in various parts.* WRNS Headquarters, London 1919.

Bigland, Eileen. *The Story of the W.R.N.S.* Nicholson & Watson, 1960.

Broome, Captain J. *Services Wrendered.* Educational Explorers, 1977.

Brown, M. and Meehan, P. *Scapa Flow.* Allen Lane, 1968.

Campbell, A. B. *Customs and Traditions of the Royal Navy.* Gale & Polden, 1956.

Coleman, E. C. *Rank and Rate. Volume II: Insignia of Royal Naval Ratings, WRNS, Royal Marines, QARRNS and Auxiliaries.* The Crowood Press, 2012.

Douie, V. *Daughters of Britain.* Douie, Oxford, 1946.

Drummond, John D. *Blue for a Girl.* W.H. Allen, 1960.

Fletcher, M. H. *The W.R.N.S.: A History of the Women's Royal Naval Service.* Batsford, 1989.

Furse, Dame Katharine. *Hearts and Pomegranates.* Peter Davies, 1940.

Goldsmith, M. *Women at War.* Lindsay Drummond, 1943.

Gregson, Paddy. *Ten Degrees Below Seaweed: A True Story of World War II Boat's Crew Wrens.* Merlin Books, 1993.

Houston, Roxane. *Changing Course: The Engaging Memoir of a Second World War Wren.* Grub Street, 2007.

Lamb, Christian. *I Only Joined for The Hat.* Bene Factum, 2007.

Mason, Ursula Stuart. *The Wrens 1917–77: A History of the Women's Royal Naval Service.* Educational Explorers, 1977.

Mathews, Dame Vera Laughton. *Blue Tapestry.* Hollis and Carter, 1948.

Miller, Lee. *Wrens in Camera.* Hollis and Carter, 1945.

Page, Gwendoline. *Growing Pains: A Teenager's War.* Book Guild, 1994.

Raynes, Rozelle. *Maid Matelot.* Nautical Publishing, 1971.

Rosskill, Captian S.W. *The Navy at War.* Collins, 1960.

Scott, P. *They Made Invasion Possible.* Hutchinson, 1944.

Spain, Nancy. *Thank You – Nelson.* Hutchinson, 1945.

Storey, Neil R. and Housego, Molly. *Women in the First World War.* Shire Publications, 2010.

Storey, Neil R. and Housego, Molly. *Women in the Second World War.* Shire Publications, 2011.

Thomas, Leslie and Bailey, Chris Howard. *W.R.N.S. in Camera.* Sutton, 2002.

Wadge, D. Collett. *Women in Uniform.* Sampson, Low Marston, 1946.

Williams, Marjorie. *My Island War: Recollections of a Wren.* Marjorie Williams, 1990.

Willson, Rosemary Curtis. *C/o G.P.O. London: With the Women's Royal Naval Service Overseas.* Hutchinson, 1949.

Women's Royal Naval Service Benevolent Trust. *70 Years of Trust.* Women's Royal Naval Service Benevolent Trust, 2012.

Fleet Mail Officer Staff, HMS *Europa*, headquarters of the Royal Naval patrol service, Lowestoft 1944.

PLACES TO VISIT

Bletchley Park, The Mansion, Bletchley Park, Sherwood Drive, Bletchley, Milton Keynes MK3 6EB. Telephone: 01908 640404. Website: www.bletchleypark.org.uk

The Churchill War Rooms, Clive Steps, King Charles Street, London SW1A 2AQ. Telephone: 020 7930 6961. Website: www.iwm.org.uk/visits/churchill-war-rooms

Devonport Naval Heritage Centre, Granby Way, Devonport, Plymouth PL1 4HG. Telephone: 01752 554200. Website: www.devonportnhc.wordpress.com

Dover Castle, Castle Hill, Dover, Kent CT16 1HU. Telephone: 01304 211067. Website: www.english-heritage.org.uk/visit/places/dover-castle

Eden Camp Museum, Malton, Yorkshire YO17 6RT. Telephone: 01653 697777. Website: www.edencamp.co.uk

The Historic Dockyard, Chatham, Kent ME4 4TE. Telephone: 01634 832028. Website: www.thedockyard.co.uk

HMS Ganges Association Museum, Victory House, Shotley Point Marina, Shotley Gate, Ipswich IP9 1QJ. Telephone: 01787 228417. Website: www.hmsgangesmuseum.com

Imperial War Museum (London), Lambeth Road, London SE1 6HZ. Telephone: 020 7416 5000. Website: www.iwm.org.uk

Milford Haven Museum, The Old Custom House, Sybil Way, The Docks, Milford Haven, Pembrokeshire, South Wales SA73 3AF. Telephone: 01646 694496. Website: www.milfordhavenmuseum.co.uk

National Maritime Museum, Greenwich, London SE10 9NF. Telephone: 020 8312 6565. Website: www.rmg.co.uk/national-maritime-museum

National Museum of the Royal Navy, HM Naval Base (PP66), Portsmouth PO1 3NH. Telephone: 023 9272 7582. Website: www.nmrn.org.uk

Royal Marines Museum, Eastney Esplanade, Southsea, Portsmouth, Hampshire PO4 9PX. Telephone: 023 9281 9385. Website: www.royalmarinesmuseum.co.uk

Royal Naval Patrol Service Museum, Europa Room,
  Sparrows Nest, Wapload Road, Lowestoft NR32 1XG.
  Telephone: 01502 586250.
  Website: www.rnpsa.co.uk/museum
Royal Navy Fleet Air Arm Museum, Fleet Air Arm Museum,
  RNAS Yeovilton, Ilchester, Somerset BA22 8HT.
  Telephone: 01935 840565.
  Website: www.fleetairarm.com
Western Approaches Museum, 1-3 Rumford Street, Liverpool,
  Merseyside L2 8SZ. Telephone: 0151 227 2008.
  Website: www.visitliverpool.com/things-to-do/
  western-approaches-museum

INDEX